ALL THE PAINTINGS OF
JAN VERMEER
VOLUME FIFTEEN
in the
Complete Library of World Art

The Complete Library of World Art

ALL THE PAINTINGS

OF JAN VERMEER

Text by VITALE BLOCH

Translated from the Italian by
MICHAEL KITSON

HAWTHORN BOOKS, INC.

Publishers · New York

Manufactured in Great Britain by Jarrold and Sons Ltd, Norwich

CONTENTS

	page
JAN VERMEER OF DELFT, LIFE AND WORK	7
BIOGRAPHICAL NOTES	26
NOTE ON VERMEER'S PAINTINGS	27
VERMEER'S PAINTINGS	29
LOCATION OF PAINTINGS	41
SELECTED CRITICISM	43
BIBLIOGRAPHICAL NOTE	49
REPRODUCTIONS	51

I have not changed the text of the small volume which was published in Italian in 1954. There have been minor alterations in the catalogue *raisonné* and some additions to the bibliography. Articles on the "Sphinx of Delft" have been appearing again and again. Of particular interest is the archival research into the posthumous auction sales which included the great majority of Vermeer's paintings. The subject-matter of his work, his musicians and especially the so-called *Artist's Studio* in Vienna has been investigated with great zest, perhaps even with too much ardor and ingenuity. The painting recently attributed to him (*The Refusal of the Glass* in the National Gallery, London) seems to me too laborious and unwieldy. Let us keep the image of Vermeer, this "Greek" painter of the Netherlands, as pure as possible.

V. B.

April 1963

JAN VERMEER OF DELFT

Life and Work

THE art of the Seven Provinces (which we call simply "Holland") had a unique place in the culture of Europe in the seventeenth century. Its character was conditioned by the geography of the country, by the Calvinist faith and by the particular mentality of the people. Having won independence from the Hapsburgs they settled down to a peaceful, *bourgeois* and hard-working way of life. Although this has often been repeated, and although it supports Taine's positivist "environment" theories, it is none the less indisputable. The Dutch concept of realism in the seventeenth century, which developed out of the universal and religious vision of the Renaissance, led, through love of simplicity, to a sub-division of the visible world into various compartments: in this way landscape, the genre picture, the church interior, still life and other categories of painting emerged. Mythological, historical and religious subjects tended to disappear, or appeared only in big official commissions—the decoration of town halls, royal palaces and other public buildings. (The timeless art of Rembrandt is of course excluded from this view of the "golden century of Dutch painting"—which in fact lasted only half a century.)

This descriptive, "documentary" form of expression employed by the Dutch painters produced a comprehensive image of the character of the country, the architecture of its cities, its domestic life and the activities and amusements of its people. In fact, if one is looking for a true and vivid idea of seventeenth-century Dutch civilization, it is inferred far better from paintings, drawings, and engravings than from written memoirs (which are scarce) or from poetry.

The realistic vision of the Dutch painters was once felt to be—in the bad sense—unimaginative and down-to-earth; but to feel this was to make the mistake of considering only the poetic, the visionary, and even the literary imagination, as "true." This was the attitude of classical historians of the seventeenth century, and up to a point it was shared in the last century by Delacroix, Baudelaire and Fromentin. The concept of the perceptual, visual imagination only emerged slowly. Rilke's "*Il ne faut pas être las et se nourrir par les yeux*" is a dictum of our time. No one today would deny Cézanne's imaginative power, although he chose to paint apples, tables with food and crockery, or Mont Sainte-Victoire. Yet the Dutch vocation for realism, for seeking and finding solutions other than through the great classic, Baroque or naturalistic modes of expression of Italy, France, Flanders and Spain, has resulted in their painting being little studied—or treated with condescension—in humanist circles; or, as with Berenson, held to be scarcely a factor of importance and almost a deviation from the main current of European art. The Dutch "chronicles" have seemed uniform and monotonous: hence the witticism of a high-minded Italian scholar—"It is as difficult to distinguish one Dutch painter from another as it is to distinguish between Japanese prints: they all look alike." The complete sympathy which a North European extends to *les petits maîtres* (even to *les plus petits maîtres*) cannot be expected from a Latin; when judging a picture the latter is accustomed to take the criticism of style as his starting-point, and above all to analyze sense of form, rather than to watch for nuances in the handling of materials, in the rendering of moods and in the representation of reality by means of equivalents.

In this sense Vermeer is not "Dutch." He stands out from among his more communicative fellow-countrymen as the great artist of silence. The liveliness of their figures contrasts with the stillness of his; their warm and lyrical chiaroscuro with his absolute clarity; the range of subtle gradations in their palette with his combination of positive local color (particularly blues and yellows). While they sought to encompass the visible world in the microcosm of their seascapes, flat, open landscapes, their panoramas of strand and dune, he preferred the close viewpoint of his *Little Street* (plate 18) and his *View of Delft* (plates 40–41). His attitude is that of the Primitives. His views of a city have the character of portraiture—or more precisely, of still life—rather than of topography. It is as still life that his sparsely peopled interiors are treated. The leather-covered chairs, the carpets, the curtains which, gathered back in folds, allow one to look into his world; the Delft jugs, the mirrors, the maps; and finally the pearls—whether as earrings or as necklaces—all these objects are essentially mute and tranquil. Yet no actual *Still Life* by Vermeer survives. What could that picture have looked like ("*een stil leven van Vermeer*") which was listed in an auction sale in 1696, the year that twenty-one pictures by him were sold? It can scarcely have resembled the lush, exotic, Baroque works of Willem Kalf, in which a gleaming lemon, a sparkling glass of wine or a bright Chinese goblet assert their predominance in the composition. Vermeer's *Still Life*—at least, so one would like to think—would be in that respect "introverted" and reserved in comparison with a Kalf. In its relation to the objects depicted, it would have the meditative, poetic harmony of, for example, Metsu (*The Jug* in the Louvre) or Anraadt (*Still Life*, formerly in the Norris Collection, now Van der Bergh Collection, The Hague).

When one sees paintings by Vermeer hanging on the same wall of the Rijksmuseum in Amsterdam as those of Brekelenkam, Pieter de Hoogh and Bisschop, one feels prompted to lift them out of so *bourgeois* a context and set them on the timeless plane of the Primitives. *The Woman in Blue* (plate 47), like the *Girl in a Turban* in The Hague (plate 49), could take its place beside a Bellini *Madonna*, the Petrus Christus *Portrait of a Young Woman* in Berlin, and perhaps even Piero della Francesca. It will be remembered that, confronting the *Madonna di Sinigallia* in Urbino, Roberto Longhi invoked the spirit of the Master of Delft. And it comes as no surprise that in recent years an affinity has been repeatedly observed between the visual approach of Vermeer and that of Jan Van Eyck: the lens-like vision, the luminous, "positive" color, the calm devoted attitude before still, silent objects—these are qualities common to both artists. Their spiritual assumptions are, of course, so different that they prevent one from pushing the comparison too far. Yet, although Vermeer first set eyes on the world exactly two centuries after the completion of Jan Van Eyck's polyptych of *The Adoration of the Mystic Lamb* in Ghent (1432), the slippers in the foreground of Vermeer's *The Love Letter* (plate 61) awaken memories of the Gothic wooden shoes in Van Eyck's *Marriage of Arnolfini* in London.

Though it seems incredible, Vermeer's art was forgotten for almost two hundred years: he died in 1675 and the earliest essays of Thoré-Bürger were published in 1866. But the oversight is less surprising than it at first appears. There was no, as we should now say, "independent" art critic in seventeenth-century Holland. The Dutch humanists, historians and poets were governed by classical prejudices and responded only to the content of a picture (historical or religious) on which they bestowed their admiration. And although the romantically colored view of Rembrandt's isolation ("the unbridgeable gulf between him and his age") has been successfully demolished, it remains true that the timeless and visionary elements of his late style in particular were never understood. The "violent," Baroque and dramatic Rembrandt of the 1630's won recognition and support from the distinguished humanist, Constantin Huygens, and he painted some scenes from the life of Christ for the Stadhouder, Frederik Hendrik; but the "purified" Rembrandt of the 1650's and 1660's, the Rembrandt who became a classic, who joined hands, as it were, with Raphael, Leonardo and Titian, was found to be incomprehensible, and his masterpiece, *The Conspiracy of Julius Civilis*, painted for the Amsterdam Town Hall and now in Stockholm, was returned to him. The greatest poet of the age, Vondel, apostrophized Rembrandt in some occasional verses and lavished praise on his pupil Govaert Flink, a conscientious follower of the "middle way," who aimed at a superficial synthesis of design and color. In the end it was an Italian collector, Don Antonio Ruffo of Messina, and two distinguished artists of the Italian Seicento, Guercino and Mattia Preti, who paid homage to Rembrandt's late style. A Fleming, Abraham Bruegel, objected to his chiaroscuro with the remark: "*Li pittori grandi studino a fayre vedere un bel corpo niudo . . .*" ("Great painters try to show a beautiful nude").

After this brief excursion into Rembrandt criticism, we may ask how could pedantic and academic historians, burdened with every possible formula for beauty, begin to approach the art of Vermeer, an art whose content was not "content" but an effect of light? And how could they deal with Vermeer's life, a life which seemed to follow a well-defined course of uninterrupted work, with no journey to Italy and nothing to satisfy the scholar's thirst for anecdote? Houbraken, who was grounded in the Vasari-Van Mander tradition, published his *groote Schouburgh* in 1718 without even giving Vermeer's name. Setting aside a few brief references during the eighteenth century (by the connoisseur, Lebrun, husband of Mme Vigée-Lebrun, and by Reynolds) which do not show any real recognition of Vermeer's importance, we have to wait until 1866, when the Frenchman, Thoré, who signed himself "Bürger" (Citizen) to indicate his radical political views, published his work on the "Sphinx of Delft." And although other French writers, such as Théophile Gautier, Maxim Decamps and the brothers Goncourt, praised Vermeer (not, however, that their observations were always accurate) it does not seem that Thoré-Bürger's discovery made much impression, since Fromentin in his *Maitres d'autrefois* (1876) gave Vermeer no place at all beyond a derogatory sentence.* Fromentin, in his evaluation of Dutch painters, started from what by modern standards were relatively academic premises; he ignored the great French contemporary movement (Impressionism) altogether and it was therefore significant that he ignored Vermeer also. It seems that the time was not yet ripe, although certain painters such as François Bonvin (1867) and Camille Pissarro (1898) spoke enthusiastically of Vermeer. At the end of the century the Dutch archivists and scholars, Obreen, Bredius and Hofstede de Groot, began to publish documents which contributed to a knowledge of Vermeer's life; and the spirited,

* See Vitale Bloch: "Fromentin, come critico," in *Paragone*, No. 1, 1950.

finely written essay on his art by the Dutch painter, Jan Veth, dates from 1908 and remains in many respects unsurpassed.

From then on all eyes were opened. Various studies followed, in particular the work of Plietzsch (1911) and Bode (1917). These, however, do not do justice to the "coolness" of Vermeer, whose art is contrasted with that of de Hoogh—"so much warmer." (In the same way James Weale in his time had preferred Memling to Van Eyck.) German writers seem to have been too occupied with spiritual truth of feeling to be able to appreciate and interpret justly the aloofness of Vermeer and the contemplative element in his art. On the whole a new climate was wanted to provide the conditions necessary to the recognition of his particular kind of beauty. The same generation which felt strongly attracted to the formal world of Piero della Francesca admired in Vermeer a new Hellenism. The development of modern painting which followed on Impressionism—particularly the work of Cézanne—contributed to this response. At the same time the great French writers influenced and enriched our ways of seeing and feeling: the relationship between form and content formulated by Valéry rendered meaningless the question of who this or that figure by Vermeer might be; and Marcel Proust taught us that art by no means represents a copy of reality, but itself creates a truer, nobler and poetic reality. Today there must be countless "Odettes" (the character in Proust) for whom Vermeer's name is "as familiar as that of their tailor."

The little we know of Vermeer's life can be summarized in a few sentences. He was baptized with the name of Johannes on October 31, 1632, in the Nieuwe Kerk ("New Church") in Delft. His father, Reynier, was an innkeeper who also dealt in pictures. Vermeer married at twenty-one, and in the same year (1653) entered the Guild of St Luke. He was elected a member of the governing body, and was also made President, at various periods (1663; 1670). He died in 1675, aged forty-three, and was buried on December 15 in the Oude Kerk ("Old Church"). Most surviving documents refer to domestic matters and we learn that he fell upon hard times particularly in the last years of his life (during the war with France); he even had to give up his activity as an art dealer. His widow, Catharina, of whose ten children eight were still under age at their father's death, had to contend with serious difficulties. We know that she settled her debts to the baker with two pictures (perhaps still unidentified) and that *An Allegory of Painting* (plate 62) was made over to the artist's mother-in-law.

It is worth recalling that in 1663 a French nobleman, Balthasar de Monconys, visited Delft and noted, "At Delft I saw the painter Vermeer, who had none of his works with him; but we saw one at the house of a baker that had been bought for six hundred *livres*, although it contained only one figure, which I should have thought expensive at six *pistoles*." It is curious that Monconys should not have found a single picture in the artist's house, since in 1696 at least twenty-one paintings from his hand were auctioned in Amsterdam, and this represents the major part of his output. The explanation may be that while Vermeer was still alive, Jac. Abrahamsz. Dissius, a Delft printer, seems to have assembled a collection of his work.

Although Vermeer's art is exceptionally uniform—still settings, still objects, still landscapes, motionless women; no children, flowers or animals with the single exception of the dog in *Diana and the Nymphs* (plate 1)—we may nevertheless try to establish a chronology. There are only a few dates to act as fixed points supporting the criteria of style and the not always reliable evidence of costume: *The Procuress* (plate 5) is dated 1656 and *The Astronomer* (plate 70), 1668.

From his joining the Guild of St Luke in 1653, Vermeer's development covers about twenty years and is continuous: the first attempts, the mature works, the zenith and the decline follow one upon the other. Let us look with particular attention at the earliest works attributed to him (those before 1656) in the hope that they will tell us something of his origins and formative period. But where shall we search for the origins of his style? *Diana and the Nymphs* is a thoughtful, balanced composition—glowing with color—which, with its meditative harmony, in a sense recalls the art of Venice; it is as if, right from the beginning, perhaps at the very moment he was accepted by the Guild, Vermeer wished to assert his place in the great European tradition. Often as the attribution has been contested, this picture of Diana is too remarkable to be fobbed off on to some anonymous little master; moreover it has characteristics which allow it to be securely associated with Vermeer's subsequent work. This painting—a mythological subject—was followed by one from the Gospels, *Christ in the House of Martha and Mary* (plate 2). This is an exercise in the contemporary Baroque manner, such as one seldom meets in Dutch paintings of these years; indeed there has been no lack of attempts (unsuccessful) to find precedents for it, especially for the figure of Christ. Finally, in the dated picture of *The Procuress* (plate 5) of 1656, Vermeer appears as an already mature artist who had come to his own understanding of reality. However uncertain he may be in space composition, he employs here a richness of color and chiaroscuro which we do not find again in his work.

Let us pause to consider these pictures, so varied in character and, for Vermeer, so unusual in theme and in their large scale, while we try to take account of his beginnings. Here, certainly, there is a literary reference to relations which may have existed between him and Carel Fabritius (1614–54), who was much the most original and independent of the followers of Rembrandt. The printer Arnold Bon composed a poem after Fabritius's tragic death—in 1654 in an explosion at Delft—in which he says toward the end: "Vermeer, as a master, perpetuated his knowledge." Pictures by Fabritius are listed in the inventory of goods left by Vermeer; and there is an undeniable spiritual affinity between Fabritius's poetic, rather melancholy conceptions—especially where they find expression in *The Goldfinch* and the *Sentry at the Gate*, both dating from the year of his death—and the sensibility of Vermeer. The connexion with Utrecht and its somewhat homespun imitation of Caravaggio is more hypothetical, though generally admitted by critics; but we are certainly at once reminded of Terbrugghen, whose pictures with their clarity and fine gradations of light—they were painted after a stay in Rome—strike us as foreshadowing Vermeer; and we may perhaps detect an echo of Terbrugghen's "soft" style in the fluid, viscous brushstroke of a picture like *Christ in the House of Martha and Mary*. However, too much weight should not be attached either to the undoubted fact that the "Procuress" theme was generally popular with the Caravaggesque painters of Utrecht, or to the presence of a rather coarse version of *The Procuress* by Dirk van Baburen on the walls of two interiors painted by Vermeer (plates 33 and 87).

Terbrugghen died in 1629. Surprisingly early—in the 1620's in fact, concurrently with Orazio Gentileschi—he had introduced into Holland an unusually modern style of painting based on tone and light values (cf. the Cassel *Flute Players*). In the following decades there occurred the often neglected period of "Haarlem classicism" (not that it was confined to Haarlem): this was a tendency toward beauty, lightness and monumentality which found expression in, for example, the work of Caesar van Everdingen for the "Huys ten Bosch" and similarly in his extraordinary still lifes.

Not only in Haarlem, but also in Utrecht (one remembers the later development of Honthorst and the other local "ex" Caravaggesque painters), in Amsterdam and other cities, the transition was completed from dark to light; from movement to stillness; from Baroque to classicism. Fabritius's *Goldfinch* on a white ground seems to proclaim a new age. And there is a sense in which Caesar van Everdingen as well as Terbrugghen can be counted among the progenitors of Vermeer.

Despite our knowledge of his very early works and our conscientious attempts to track down his predecessors; despite the "painting of light values" in Utrecht and the classicism of Haarlem; despite the luminous backgrounds and the lyric quality of Fabritius; despite the subtle experiments with space carried out by the painters of church interiors who were either born in Delft or worked there for a time (Van Vliet, Houckgeest and above all Emanuel de Witte)—despite all these, the paintings by Vermeer which follow *The Procuress* come upon one like a revelation. How should one arrange them in chronological order? There have been attempts to establish such an order, although it is something which can be treated only in its main outlines; and the question "When was it painted?" naturally has meaning only in so far as it seeks to throw light on Vermeer's artistic development.

At the beginning of the series, on the threshold of this rarefied world, stands *A Lady Reading a Letter by the Window* in Dresden (plate 12). Here we meet for the first time the profile of a young woman—on this occasion reading a letter—"detached" from a high, bare wall; here Vermeer already attains the peace and equilibrium, the clarity which distinguishes his work. The hanging, the curtain, the carpet, the chair and the blue fruit bowl accompany the letter reader, as it were, like mute supporting players. We shall continually meet these silent objects; they are not secondary; there was no hierarchy for Vermeer. The picture is remarkable for its warm coloring and it already shows the artist's characteristic technique—his use of little dots and granules.

A Soldier and Laughing Girl (plate 14) belongs to that group of specific genre paintings (dialogues between a man and a woman or between a woman and girl) in which Vermeer associated himself, outwardly at least, with tradition. The striking silhouette of the soldier, which somehow seems to evoke Holland's glorious past, does not recur; but the map on the wall—a kind of *invitation au voyage*—belongs to the chosen repertory of the artist. In *The Milkmaid* (plate 16) he attains a solemn, almost monumental grandeur and his Pointillism finds its culminating expression in the still life of the kitchen. Who else ever painted a common milkmaid with so much seriousness and concentration?

We may presume that the two "landscapes" also belong to a relatively early period, though perhaps with an interval of a few years between them. But is *The Little Street* (plate 18) really a city view? It is, rather, an interior turned out-of-doors; or more precisely, a still life. In the whole range of Dutch—and probably of European—painting in the seventeenth century, *The Little Street* has no equal. Max Liebermann who, like Degas, was a connoisseur of painting, described it as being the most beautiful of all easel pictures. A simple, anonymous motif, a brick façade, becomes poetry and assumes a permanent value. It is a picture which represents a climax in the artistic heritage of Holland: it has become a symbol of Dutch painting.

The *View of Delft* (plates 40–41) is more spacious in composition, more radiant and gay in color and lighting. The city, with its roofs, gate-house and towers, is silhouetted against the great arc of the sky; the sun breaks through and illuminates the center and right side of the composition, while the left remains in shadow. Blue, red and yellow in varying gradations harmonize with one another. Only the trees, which have turned blue in the course of time, disturb the impression. The Pointillist technique gives the color pattern the character of embroidery, at the same time recalling the glazed enamel of Oriental ceramics. The historian seeks in vain for precedents for, or parallels with, this motionless and, as it were, crystallized view. One can imagine the impression made on Thoré by such an orchestra of color—so striking among the general monochrome of Dutch landscape painting. And memories of the "little strip of yellow wall" seem also to have haunted Proust.

Other genre paintings group themselves round *A Soldier and Laughing Girl*, some of which—*The Music Lesson* (plate 24) and *A Girl with a Glass of Wine and Two Gentlemen* (plate 26)—have a flavor which, however discreet, tends to disturb the equilibrium of the composition and conflicts with the "still life" character of Vermeer's form: when his women move or look out of the frame we feel uncomfortable. It seems difficult to establish any indisputable chronology among these "conversation pieces." If, like some biographer, one relies primarily on the evidence of costume, then the music scenes in Buckingham Palace and Boston—*A Gentleman and Lady at a Spinet* (plate 27) and *The Concert* (plate 33)—are early works, associable with *A Lady Reading a Letter by the Window* and *A Soldier and Laughing Girl*.

Then follow the true *scènes galantes*, like *A Girl Drinking with a Gentleman* (plate 22), *The Music Lesson* (plate 24) and *A Girl with a Glass of Wine* (plate 26), the last of these appearing to be the latest of the group. But if instead we consider primarily the main stylistic evolution, then *The Concert* (plate 33) and *A Gentleman and Lady at a Spinet*, which takes us over into the mature period of the 1660's, belong at the end and not at the beginning of the series. Briefly then, the *scènes galantes* form a special enclave within Vermeer's development.

The most expressive picture of this group seems to be *A Gentleman and Lady at a Spinet*, in which space becomes the subject while the two figures stand in the distance against the background: the woman with her back turned, the man at her side. Like a Quattrocento artist, Vermeer seeks by every possible means to encompass the third dimension. After the heavy folds of the tablecloth come the double bass and the obliquely placed chair: and, as in *The Marriage of Arnolfini* by Van Eyck, a mirror is fixed to the back wall, reflecting the head of the woman and part of the tiled floor. Those who need an explanation of the content of the picture will find it in the writing on the lid of the virginals: "*Musica letitiae comes medicina dolor(um)*."

Not the collocation of two or more figures, however abstractly and separately conceived, but the representation of a single figure—of a young woman, for the man is only an accompaniment—is the recurring theme of Vermeer's art: he expressed woman's passive, introspective nature before Watteau, Gainsborough or Renoir. These figures at times resemble each other so closely that they have become indistinguishable: *A Young Woman with a Water Jug* (plate 35), *A Woman Weighing Pearls* (plate 38), *The Woman in Blue* (plate 47), *A Lady Reading a Letter by the Window* (plate 12).

André Malraux believed that the artist's wife was represented in all of them—and one of his daughters in the *Girl in a Turban* (plate 49)—and constructed on this basis a chronology which cannot, however, be proved. In these pictures Vermeer renounces action and movement altogether, except that which is only implied or is of a contemplative nature. What is *A Young Woman with a Water Jug* really doing? The women in the pictures in Berlin (plate 50) and Washington (plate 38) are absorbed with the pearls: *The Woman in Blue* (plate 47) is preoccupied with her letter. Maps on the walls, precious boxes, trays, jugs, Chinese vases adorn the settings. We do not ask "when?" or "where?" With these pictures we are outside time. The light becomes diffused, the shadows transparent. There is everywhere less red and green: blues and yellows dominate the palette. It is impossible to decide among this group of figures which forms the most beautiful picture: but that the most familiar —*The Woman in Blue*—is a masterpiece, is altogether beyond doubt.

The *Girl in a Turban* in The Hague is weighed down by her own fame. If only one could see her again for the first time! She has been called—probably in allusion to her celebrity—the "Gioconda of the North." A less appropriate description could scarcely have been thought of. For it is in the essentially still-life character of this child's head that the magic of the picture resides. She looks at us with large wide eyes: her expression suggests simply "be at peace." The basic color harmony is blue and yellow, the delicate surface of the painting seeming to be made of "a fusion of crushed pearls," in Jan Veth's phrase. It is an apt comparison.

An Allegory of Painting (plate 62) permits us a view into the studio of an artist painting on canvas the figure of a woman who symbolizes perhaps fame or perhaps the Muse, Clio. (It will be noted that his method is to fill in with color the part which he has drawn on the canvas beforehand.) The question if the figure of the artist is a self-portrait cannot be answered. Nevertheless, the picture is in every respect auto-biographical: we see how the artist has placed the easel close to the model, how he has posed her—she has the features of The Hague *Girl in a Turban*—in front of a map, lit as usual from the left, and so on. It is as if Vermeer were showing us how Vermeer painted a "Vermeer." In a sense *An Allegory of Painting*, which is generally dated about 1665, is one of his most highly finished works, and as such it has always been admired. But we may ask whether the perfection of its technique does not in itself conceal a dangerous tendency. "Its style is throughout like an unruffled sheet of water, but one which no longer reflects the emotions of the human heart," remarked Johansen.

An excess of skill spoils Vermeer's last works. He painted exquisite pictures—*The Lacemaker* (plate 54), *The Love Letter* (plate 58) and others—but they show a decline in intensity of poetic feeling and one misses the amazing detachment of the earlier Vermeer. The women follow the fashion in dress and hair style, and when they play a musical instrument they look out at the spectator. We are on the edge of merely "fine painting." And Vermeer foundered when he painted, perhaps on commission, the ambitious *Allegory of Faith* (plate 79). This is a picture more in the style of Leyden than of Delft. Not even its beautiful parts, especially the curtain, can compensate for the absence of imagination and inventiveness. Mind and matter are in conflict.

Let us glance once more at Vermeer's work as a whole. After a few irrelevant experiments, he found a personal style: he created works in which form and color unite in a wonderful harmony. The imaginative structure of these works is unique: *The Little Street, A Young Woman with a Water Jug, The Woman in Blue*, the *Girl in a Turban*, the *View of Delft* and others. *An Allegory of Painting* perhaps represents the culminating expression of his feeling for order. The pictures which are believed to date from between 1665 and 1670, like *A Lady Writing a Letter and her Maid* (plate 74) and *The Love Letter* (plate 58), depend upon an excess of technique and upon skill in illusionism: they come near to *trompe-l'œil*, and it has been suggested that even in the preceding works Vermeer had recourse to some mechanical device. In the interiors—(the paintings in London) *A Young Woman Standing at a Virginal* (plate 81) and *A Young Woman Seated at a Virginal* (plate 85)—he withheld even the magic of color.

Art critics have applied all their intelligence and acumen in an attempt to imprison the phenomenon which is Vermeer in a web of "parallels," "influences," etc.—but the attempt is a vain one. If the classical historians ignored Vermeer, the scientific art historians have been frustrated. Baffled, they seem to have abandoned him to the poets and men of letters: Marcel Proust, Louis Gillet, Paul Claudel and André Malraux have all found themselves attracted to his art. Yet, in speaking of Vermeer, Claudel resorted to English words—"eerie," "uncanny"—as if his own language were inadequate; and René Huyghe, in a brilliant essay entitled *La Poétique de Vermeer*, attempted a synthesis between the criticism and the psychology of art.

Vermeer undermines all the hard and fast traditional concepts of the various categories in Dutch paintings: thus in his genre scenes nothing happens (one never knows what title to give his pictures), while his city landscapes are treated essentially as still lifes. For this reason it is unrewarding to compare his still, silent world with the world of other contemporary Dutch genre painters. Are there relations with Steen and Pieter de Hoogh, who worked for a time in Delft (Steen from 1654 to 1660, de Hoogh from 1649 to 1657)? A shade of color, a gesture, a motif may correspond but never the essentials. One need only recall de Hoogh's variations on the theme of *A Woman Weighing Pearls*: compared with Vermeer's, his cosy and sentimental interiors appear weak and inconsistent. Vermeer's art is to that of his contemporaries as a poem is to prose narrative.

The comparison with Metsu or Terborch is no more valid than that with Steen or de Hoogh. Whereas Steen contrasts with Vermeer in the energy and inventive quality of his figure style, Metsu (1629–67) sinks to the "fine painting" characteristic of Leyden, even though at times, as in the *Still Life* in the Louvre and the sensitive *Sick Child* in Amsterdam, he achieved something exceptional. The pictures by him in the Beit Collection (*The Letter Reader, The Boy Writing*), which ostensibly owe their formal language to Vermeer, are pure products of the Leyden approach. Terborch (1617–81) possessed an unmistakable personality; he could create an effect of grandeur on a small scale; and some of his genre scenes show remarkable taste and sensitivity. But although his female figures sometimes appear in profile—when they are not actually with their backs to the spectator—and although it is not always possible to discover what is happening in his pictures, his art nevertheless remains essentially illustrative, narrative and the antithesis of Vermeer's in its formal idiom. It is in Terborch, whose works are endlessly varied, that we find reflected the fundamental distinction between "fine paintings" and "Vermeer"; between prose narrative and poetry.

Deceptive, because external and superficial, comparisons

between the subject-matter of Vermeer and that of his contemporaries (F. van Mieris, Metsu, Nicolas Maes, Pieter de Hoogh, Caspar Netscher, Pieter Janssens Elinga), who always tended to "illustrate" something, are less rewarding than attempts to see his painting of light values in a wider context; to see it in relation to the vision and language of form developed in Rome in the first decades of the seventeenth century by Caravaggio, Elsheimer and their followers; by Orazio Gentileschi and Terbrugghen.

It is hopeless to try to resolve the ultimate mystery of this enigmatic artist. One always feels that he is "a hummingbird among sparrows," in Friedlander's phrase. Perhaps his art is more intelligible if it is conceived not as an exception in contrast with its background but rather as the quintessence and synthesis of the Dutch character, of the Dutch taste for everything that is polished, succinct, clean, bright and spotless; as the sublimation of the surfaces of things, of their still and silent life, of their motionless existence.

In the end Vermeer's significance lies in this: that he strove to translate the "here and now" into the sphere of an enchanted stillness, into the "above and beyond," where Rembrandt sought to make the "above and beyond" universally comprehensible.

BIOGRAPHICAL NOTES

1632, OCTOBER 31. Baptized in the Nieuwe Kerk in Delft.

1653, APRIL 5. Married Catharina Bolenes of Gouda.

1653, DECEMBER 29. Admitted to the Guild of St Luke as a "master."

1656. Date of *The Procuress* in Dresden.

1662. Elected a member of the governing body of the Guild of St Luke.

1663. Elected President of the Guild of St Luke.

1668. Date of *The Astronomer* (in the Rothschild Collection).

1669. Mentioned for the second time as a member of the governing body of the Guild of St Luke.

1670. Elected President of the Guild of St Luke for the second time.

1672. Called in as an expert to give his opinion on a large number of Italian pictures at The Hague.

1675, DECEMBER 15. Buried in the Oude Kerk in Delft.

1688. Death of his widow.

1696, MAY 16. Twenty-one pictures from his hand sold at auction in Amsterdam.

NOTE ON VERMEER'S PAINTINGS

The following catalogue contains only works whose attribution to Vermeer can be considered certain. In two cases (*A Girl with a Red Hat* and *A Girl with a Flute*, both in Washington) some legitimate doubt has been expressed. However, without examining the paintings again I cannot decide to cancel them arbitrarily from my "lists."

Before the war there was a tendency—on the part of Hofstede de Groot (1930), E. Plietzsch and A. B. De Vries (1939) especially—to enlarge the œuvre of Vermeer, a tendency which was general among connoisseurs at that time. Much was "found" and there were many "revelations"; but so widely cast a net inevitably landed only a few really big fish. This desire to extend at all costs the small output of Vermeer (thus diluting the few certain works) manifested itself in various ways. Alien, though fine and artistically valuable works, were hurriedly "rescued" from anonymity and assigned to him. One recalls in particular the expressive portrait of a Slavonic-looking woman in Budapest, which was accepted by all the connoisseurs as the unique portrait in the Vermeer canon (Plietzsch, 1939, No. 36, plate 12). Such a painting, if executed by Vermeer, would have to belong to a hypothetical Rembrandtesque phase and to be closely associated with Fabritius.

But more recently, works of no real importance—though remarkable enough in composition—have been put forward as possible Vermeers. Some of these can be attributed to the Haarlem artist Van Blommendael (see the present author's article in *Oud-Holland*, 1940, pp. 17–21). The *Portrait of a Man Reading* has always seemed to me to be more in the spirit of Haarlem than of Delft (not only on account of Casteleijn's drawing after it in the Welcker Collection, Amsterdam), and it is scarcely possible to understand how so experienced a scholar as Plietzsch can have published it as a Vermeer (No. 33 in his catalogue). A. B. De Vries, who previously shared Plietzsch's opinion no longer accepts the picture in the revised (1948) edition of his book.

The problem of the fake Vermeers with which the pre-war biographers enriched the œuvre is more delicate. But in recent monographs—De Vries (1948), Swillens (1950), Gowing (1952) and Malraux (1952)—the genuine has been separated from the false. One could indeed write a treatise on the various types of Vermeer forgery. The easiest to recognize are, of course, those which are (very clumsily) made up of a sort of anthology of motifs from genuine pictures: (for example, the *Music Lesson*, formerly in the Mannheimer Collection, the forty-first reproduction in the De Vries *Supplement*, 1948). What appear to be two caricatures of authentic pictures belong to the National Gallery in Washington (see again De Vries—plates 35 and

38). In a fit of youthful enthusiasm the author of the present catalogue identified (*Cicerone*, 1928) a small *Letter Reader* as a genuine work (Bache Collection, New York).

This is not the place to reopen the problem of the celebrated forgeries by Van Meegeren. The author's opinions can be found in *L'Amour de l'Art*, 1946, "Van Meegeren, Faussaire de Vermeer." Having awarded a laurel to the *Supper at Emmaus* (Boymans Museum, Rotterdam) which is surprisingly well executed technically (though wholly uncharacteristic of the seventeenth century in feeling, being attuned rather to modern "psychological" attitudes), then one cannot but give a lesser honor—however unwillingly and against one's instincts—to the *Magdalene at the Feet of the Redeemer* which the Dutch nation bought during the last war. There is no need to dwell on the rest of Van Meegeren's concoctions.

A word about Vermeer drawings. The *Study of a Head* in the Kupferstichkabinett in Berlin has been attributed to him by Plietzsch (Plietzsch, 1939, plate 15); this is understandable if one accepts the *Head of a Woman* in Budapest. Professor van Regteren Altena has given some reasons in favor of Vermeer's authorship of the *Girl Asleep under a Tree* (*Hollandische Meisterzeichnungen des 17en Jahrhunderts*, Basel, 1948, plate 43), and lately he has connected a drawing of St Francis in his own collection with the head of Christ in the painting in Edinburgh. These drawings are rather indifferent. How *did* Vermeer draw? We shall never know.

VERMEER'S PAINTINGS

Color Plate I
DIANA AND THE NYMPHS. Detail of plate 1.

Plate 1
DIANA AND THE NYMPHS. *Canvas, 98.5 × 105*. The Hague, Mauritshuis.* Signed. Early work, before 1656. The picture was acquired for the Mauritshuis in Paris in 1876. It bore the (false) signature of Nicolas Maes. With some exceptions (Swillens has suggested the artist's father, Reynier Vos, alias Vermeer, as the author of the picture, which he identified with No. 55 in the auction sale held in Amsterdam on May 16, 1696), it is generally agreed to be an autograph work by Vermeer himself. There are evident relationships with the signed *Christ in the House of Martha and Mary* (see comment on plate 2). As Jan Veth pointed out, one can detect certain qualities characteristic of Vermeer's subsequent work in the balance of the composition and in the poses of some of the figures. A composition on the same theme by Jacob van Loo, of which there are versions in Berlin and Copenhagen, has been suggested as a precedent for the picture. Since the cleaning in 1952 the signature has appeared more clearly.

Plate 2
CHRIST IN THE HOUSE OF MARTHA AND MARY. *Canvas, 159 × 141. Edinburgh, National Gallery of Scotland.* Signed IVMeer.

Early work, before 1656. Various precedents have been suggested for the figure of Christ: a comparison has often been made with the corresponding figure in the *Death of St Joseph* by Andrea Vaccaro in the Naples Museum. But this relationship, like that with the figure of Christ by Alessandro Allori in Vienna or by Erasmus Quellinus in Valenciennes, is superficial.

Swillens denies the authenticity of the picture and attributes it to Johan van der Meer of Utrecht, about whom we know almost nothing. Because of a similarity in the drapery of the figure of Mary, Professor van Regteren Altena has tentatively attributed to Vermeer a red chalk drawing of a *Girl Asleep under a Tree* (39.5 × 44.5) which is in a private collection in Amsterdam: he has published this in his *Hollandische Meisterzeichnungen des 17en Jahrhunderts*, Basle, 1948.

Plate 3
CHRIST IN THE HOUSE OF MARTHA AND MARY. Detail: Martha.

Plate 4
CHRIST IN THE HOUSE OF MARTHA AND MARY. Detail: Mary.

Plate 5
THE PROCURESS. *Canvas, 143 × 130. Dresden, Gemäldegalerie.* Signed IVMeer and dated 1656. The subject of venal love was popular with the

* All dimensions are given in centimeters.

Utrecht painters. The version by Dirk van Baburen (of which two replicas are known, in Amsterdam and Boston) hangs on the walls of two of Vermeer's own interiors: *The Concert* (plate 33) and *A Young Woman Seated at a Virginal* (plate 85). The comparison which used to be drawn here—perhaps over-emphasized—was with Rembrandt: the figure of the young man in a cap on the left in particular gave this some substance. René Huyghe and F. van Thienen believe the figure to be a self-portrait. (See also plates 6–8.)

Plate 6
THE PROCURESS. Detail: the young man drinking (believed by some to be a self-portrait) and the procuress.

Plate 7
THE PROCURESS. Detail: the cavalier and the harlot.

Plate 8
THE PROCURESS. Detail of still life and hands.

Plate 9
A GIRL ASLEEP. *Canvas, 85 × 73.5. New York, Metropolitan Museum of Art.* Signed IVMEER. Datable between 1655 and 1660. Number 8 in the auction sale at Amsterdam in 1696. A relatively early work, since the representation of space seems to have given the artist some difficulty. The view through into the second room, characteristic of de Hoogh, is unusual in Vermeer. The girl's cap was out of fashion by this time. The lower corner of a picture of a *Standing Cupid* tentatively attributed to Caesar van Everdingen, is visible on the wall behind the girl's head. This picture (but without the mask which can just be seen here) reappears entire in the two interiors repro-

duced in plates 24 and 81: *The Music Lesson* and *A Young Woman Standing at a Virginal*. (See also plates 10 and 11.)

Plate 10
A GIRL ASLEEP. Detail: the girl.

Plate 11
A GIRL ASLEEP. Detail: still life.

Plate 12
A LADY READING A LETTER BY THE WINDOW. *Canvas, 83 × 64.5. Dresden, Gemäldegalerie.* Traces of a signature. Datable between 1655 and 1660. Belongs at the beginning of Vermeer's classic series of female figures. Swillens points out that the standing position of the letter reader is contrary to Vermeer's usual practice, since the vanishing-point is high, above the eye level of the figure represented. (See also plate 13.)

Plate 13
A LADY READING A LETTER BY THE WINDOW. Detail: the lady and her reflection in the window-pane.

Plate 14
A SOLDIER AND LAUGHING GIRL. *Canvas, 48 × 43. New York, Frick Collection.* Datable between 1655 and 1660. Number 11 in the auction at Amsterdam in 1696. The girl's dress is identical with that in the preceding picture, as is the Pointillist technique. On the wall is a map of Holland and West Friesland, with the following inscription: NOVA ET ACCURATA TOTIUS HOLLANDIAE WESTFRISIAE (QUE) TOPOGRAPHIA (PER NICOLAUM PISCATOREM) ("A new and accurate map of the whole of Holland and West Friesland by Nicolaus Piscatores"). Part of the same map also appears in *The Woman in Blue* (plate 47). (See also plate 15.)

Plate 15

A SOLDIER AND LAUGHING GIRL.
Detail: the girl.

Plate 16

THE MILKMAID. *Canvas, 45.5 × 41. Amsterdam, Rijksmuseum.* Formerly in the Six Collection. Datable between 1655 and 1660. Number 2 in the Amsterdam auction of 1696. Mentioned by Reynolds in his account of his journey to Flanders and Holland in 1781. The dating of the picture has sometimes been questioned: Malraux believes that it belongs to a later period. Vermeer composed here an entire still life from loaves of bread, a basket, an earthenware jug, an earthenware bowl and a milk jug. (See also plate 17 and color plate II.)

Color Plate II

THE MILKMAID. Detail of plate 16.

Plate 17

THE MILKMAID. Detail: still life.

Plate 18

THE LITTLE STREET. *Canvas, 54 × 44. Amsterdam, Rijksmuseum.* Formerly in the Six Collection. Signed IVMEER. Datable between 1655 and 1660. Number 32 in the Amsterdam auction of 1696. Swillens has established that the house represented is the hostel for old women on the Voldersgracht, which Vermeer could have seen from his window before the premises of the Guild of St Luke were built there in 1661. The greens of the trees have turned blue in the course of time. (See also plates 19–21.)

Plate 19

THE LITTLE STREET. Detail.

Plate 20

THE LITTLE STREET. Detail: bottom left.

Plate 21

THE LITTLE STREET. Detail: bottom right.

Plate 22

A GIRL DRINKING WITH A GENTLEMAN. *Canvas, 66 × 76. Berlin, Staatliches Museen.* Datable between 1655 and 1660. When the picture was acquired by the Staatliches Museen (then the Kaiser Friedrich Museum) the window had been painted over and the whole composition adjusted to approximate it to the style of Terborch (the motif of the woman drinking a glass of wine is, admittedly, common in Terborch's work). On the wall in the background is a landscape in the style of Albert van Everdingen. (See also plate 23.)

Plate 23

A GIRL DRINKING WITH A GENTLEMAN. Detail.

Plate 24

THE MUSIC LESSON. *Canvas, 39 × 45. New York, Frick Collection.* Datable between 1655 and 1660. The painting is not in perfect condition: the folds of the woman's dress have been retouched and the birdcage is probably a later addition. The picture on the background wall, a *Standing Cupid*, attributed to Caesar van Everdingen, is the same as that which appeared previously in *A Girl Asleep* and which reappears in *A Young Woman Standing at a Virginal* (plates 9 and 81; see also plate 25).

Plate 25

THE MUSIC LESSON. Detail: the girl.

Plate 26

A GIRL WITH A GLASS OF WINE AND TWO GENTLEMEN. *Canvas, 78 × 67. Brunswick, Herzog Anton Ulrich Museum.* Signed IVMⲈer. Datable about 1660. The picture has suffered: the blue is streaked and so has upset the color harmony; the unpleasant smirk on the faces of both the girl and the man bending over her are due to restorations. On the wall in the background is an un-identified portrait in the style of H. C. van Vliet.

Plate 27

A GENTLEMAN AND LADY AT A SPINET. *Canvas, 73.5 × 64. London, Buckingham Palace.* Datable about 1660. Number 6 in the Amsterdam auction in 1696. In the eighteenth century this work was part of the collection of Consul Smith in Venice and was acquired together with the whole collection by George III in 1762. It is identical in size with *The Concert* in Boston (plate 33), and evidently formed a pair with it. The lady's dress has often been said to correspond with that of the figures in the relatively early *A Lady Reading a Letter by the Window* (plate 12) and *A Soldier and Laughing Girl* (plate 14). However, *A Gentleman and Lady at a Spinet* has sometimes been dated later. The inscription on the instrument reads: MUSICA LETITIAE COMES MEDICINA DOLOR(UM). Part of a picture of a *Caritas Romana* is visible on the wall at the right. The picture has recently been cleaned by the late H. Buttery. (See also plates 28–32.)

Plate 28

A GENTLEMAN AND LADY AT A SPINET. Detail: the lady and the mirror.

Plate 29

A GENTLEMAN AND LADY AT A SPINET. Detail: the gentleman.

Plate 30

A GENTLEMAN AND LADY AT A SPINET. Detail: the windows.

Plate 31

A GENTLEMAN AND LADY AT A SPINET. Detail: the carpet, the chair, the double bass and part of the tiled floor.

Plate 32

A GENTLEMAN AND LADY AT A SPINET. Detail: the lady.

Plate 33

THE CONCERT. *Canvas, 71 × 63. Boston, Isabella Stewart Gardner Museum.* Datable about 1660. Acquired by Bernard Berenson on his own initiative in 1892 for Mrs Gardner at the Thoré-Bürger Sale. On the back wall, an unidentified landscape and *The Procuress* by Dirk van Baburen (see comment to plate 5 above): this also appears in *A Young Woman Seated at a Virginal* (plates 85 and 87). (See also plate 34.)

Plate 34

THE CONCERT. Detail: the lady playing the instrument.

Plate 35

A YOUNG WOMAN WITH A WATER JUG. *Canvas, 44 × 39. New York, Metropolitan Museum of Art.* Datable about 1660, but on grounds of costume dated earlier by some scholars. To interpret the woman's gesture as an indication that she is about to water some flowers outside the window—this is a common inter-pretation—is quite arbitrary, and seems to stem from an impulse to find some "point" to the painting. (See also plates 36 and 37.)

Plate 36
A YOUNG WOMAN WITH A WATER JUG. Detail: the woman.

Plate 37
A YOUNG WOMAN WITH A WATER JUG. Detail: a hand and still life.

Plate 38
A WOMAN WEIGHING PEARLS. *Canvas, 42 × 35.5. Washington, D.C., National Gallery of Art.* Datable between 1660 and 1665. Number 1 in the auction at Amsterdam in 1696. The work is related to *The Pearl Necklace* (plate 50) more in its composition than in its color effects. Malraux thinks he sees in the figure —and also in the figure in the previous painting—a representation of the artist's wife, Catharina. On the wall is an unidentified picture of *The Last Judgement*—a "memento" to the lady who beguiles time with pearls. *The Gold Weigher* by Pieter de Hoogh in the Staatliches Museen in Berlin, which is generally thought to have been inspired by Vermeer and which has been dated by Valentiner about 1664, is a perfect example of the translation into concrete, genre terms of Vermeer's distinctive *sub specie aeternitatis* conception. (See also plate 39.)

Plate 39
A WOMAN WEIGHING PEARLS. Detail: the figure.

Plates 40–41
VIEW OF DELFT. *Canvas, 98.5 × 117.5. The Hague, Mauritshuis.* Signed IVM. Datable about 1660. Number 31 in the auction at Amsterdam in 1696. The city is seen from across the Rotterdam Canal: the Schliedam Gate is in the center, the Rotterdam Gate on the right. In the background on the right, the tower of the Nieuwe Kerk, in which Vermeer

was baptized; on the left the spire of the Oude Kerk, in which he was buried, can be seen above the roofs. Swillens believes that, as in the case of *The Little Street* (plate 18), Vermeer must have painted his view of the city from nature from the upper window of a house, which was an unusual practice in the seventeenth century.

A male figure in the foreground— it is to the right of the two women— which Vermeer had painted out, is now visible again. Due to the absorption of the yellows the trees have turned blue in the course of time. And due to the dirty yellow varnish the picture now appears considerably altered. As early as 1842 it made a great impression on Thoré-Bürger and can be regarded as the starting-point of his study of Vermeer. It also had an unforgettable effect on the French writers and painters after Thoré-Bürger, particularly Marcel Proust. The painting was cleaned in 1956. (See also plates 42–45.)

Plate 42
VIEW OF DELFT. Detail: center.

Plate 43
VIEW OF DELFT. Detail: right-hand side.

Plate 44
VIEW OF DELFT. Detail: the boats on the right.

Plate 45
VIEW OF DELFT. Detail: the foreground, bottom left.

Plate 46
HEAD OF A GIRL. *Canvos, 45 × 40. New York, Mr and Mrs Charles B. Wrighton Collection.* Formerly in the Duke of Arenberg Collection, Brussels. Signed IVMEER. Datable

between 1660 and 1665. Number 39 in the Amsterdam auction of 1696. Thoré-Bürger wrote of this work, "*Tête fantastique et pâle.*" The author has not personally seen the picture.

Plate 47

THE WOMAN IN BLUE. *Canvas, 46.5 × 39. Amsterdam, Rijksmuseum.* Datable between 1660 and 1665. Some of Vermeer's biographers believe that the woman, who is obviously pregnant, is his wife. "In the way in which the softly painted jacket of aquamarine blue, with its milk-white highlights, opens glistening like a fragrant calyx from the embrace of the deep blue chairs, this work is unique even in Vermeer" (Plietzsch). Van Gogh wrote to Emile Bernard in July 1888, on *The Woman in Blue*: "*Connais-tu un peintre nommé Vermeer qui, par example, a peint une dame hollandaise très belle, enceinte?*" Hanging on the wall is part of the same map which appears in its entirety in *A Soldier and Laughing Girl.* (See also plate 48.)

Plate 48

THE WOMAN IN BLUE. Detail.

Color Plate III

GIRL IN A TURBAN. *Canvas, 46.5 × 40. The Hague, Mauritshuis.* Signed IVMEER. Datable between 1660 and 1665. Number 38 in the Amsterdam auction of 1696. Acquired for two and a half florins by an amateur at a sale in The Hague in 1882, and presented by him to the Mauritshuis in 1903. Malraux believes that the figure represented is one of Vermeer's daughters and concludes that the picture was therefore painted at the beginning of the 1670's. But even apart from the stylistic evidence, which contradicts so late a dating, Malraux has reached a wrong conclusion: the girl in the picture could be about seven or eight years old, and hence the picture would have been painted—which seems likely—about 1665.

This masterpiece—"*étoile consolatrice qui plane au grand ciel nocturne*" (Jan Veth)—seems to have been executed somewhere about the middle of the artist's career when his creative powers were at their zenith. It belongs to the "inner circle" of his œuvre, in which the still-life character of his art found its clearest form. Jan Veth, Léon Daudet, Louis Gillet and many others have sought to elucidate the strange expression on this face, its artistic quality and the "*émail virginal et caressant de la matière*" (Gillet). The painting was cleaned in 1959–60. (See also plate 49.)

Plate 49

GIRL IN A TURBAN. Detail: the face.

Plate 50

THE PEARL NECKLACE. *Canvas, 55 × 45. Berlin, Staatliches Museen.* Signed IVMEER. Datable about 1665. Number 36 in the Amsterdam auction of 1696. From the Thoré-Bürger Collection. Entered the Staatliches Museen (then the Kaiser Friedrich Museum) with the Suermondt Collection in 1879. It is the only work by Vermeer in which the figure stands in front of a plain white wall—though it does seem that there was once a picture or a map in the upper right corner, later painted out —perhaps by Vermeer himself. (See also plate 51.)

Plate 51

THE PEARL NECKLACE. Detail: the face.

Plate 52

THE LUTE PLAYER. *Canvas, 52 × 46. New York, Metropolitan Museum of Art.* Signed MEER. Datable about 1665. Possibly this work can be identified with No. 4 in the Amsterdam auction of 1696: but the number may also refer to *The Guitar Player* at Kenwood House, London (plate 67).

Plate 53

A LADY WRITING A LETTER. *Canvas, 46 × 36. Nassau (Bahamas), Lady Oakes Collection.* Signed IVMEER. Datable about 1665. Probably Number 35 in the Amsterdam auction of 1696. The *Still Life with Musical Instruments* on the wall has recently been attributed (Kjell Boström in *Oud-Holland*, 1951) to the rare painter Cornelis van der Meulen: this artist was a pupil of S. van Hoogstraten, two portraits by whom were listed in the inventory of Vermeer's possessions.

Plate 54

THE LACEMAKER. *Canvas, 24 × 21. Paris, Louvre.* Signed IVMEER. Datable between 1665 and 1670. Number 12 in the Amsterdam auction of 1696. The hair style suggests a relatively late period. *The Lacemaker* recalls *A Lady Writing a Letter and Her Maid* in the Beit Collection (plate 74). Worth noting are the play of light and shadow, the use of little dots of color—as in earlier pictures—and the deep concentration of the woman. (See also plate 55.)

Plate 55

THE LACEMAKER. Detail: the head.

Plate 56

A GIRL WITH A RED HAT. *Canvas, 23 × 18. Washington, D.C., National Gallery of Art (Mellon Collection).*

Signed IVM. Like its pendant, *A Girl with a Flute* (plate 57), the authenticity of this painting has been doubted by Swillens and Gudlaugsson. The painting is alleged to have appeared in an auction sale in 1882 under the title, *Portrait of a Young Man.* X-rays show that the woman is painted over a vaguely Rembrandtesque portrait of a man.

Plate 57

A GIRL WITH A FLUTE. *Panel, 20 × 18. Washington, D.C., National Gallery of Art (Widener Collection)*. Discovered in Brussels by Dr. A. Bredius. It is the only known picture by Vermeer that is painted on panel. In a sense it gives the impression of being a fragment and, like the closely related *Girl with a Red Hat*, it is difficult to place in the chronology of Vermeer's work. Doubts have been openly expressed about the authenticity of both pictures: these doubts are understandable in view of the essentially strange appearance of the two figures. Johansen believed that it was possible to explain the "complete absence of expression and human emotion" by the fact that what we are looking at is only an underpainting; that the final touches are missing. Swillens mentions neither picture in his catalogue. Gudlaugsson, whose knowledge of Dutch seventeenth-century genre painting is unequalled, is very sceptical. So is Gerson.

Plate 58

THE LOVE LETTER. *Canvas, 44 × 38.5. Amsterdam, Rijksmuseum.* Signed IVMEER. Datable between 1665 and 1670. A classic example of Vermeer's late style. It will be remembered that Thoré-Bürger called him a *"faïencier de génie"*. The piece of stamped and gilded leather listed in the inventory of Vermeer's possessions is attached to the back wall in the picture. Metsu's version of the same subject in the Beit Collection seems involved and over-detailed in comparison with Vermeer's "mathematical" conception. The pictures hanging on the back wall are a landscape, only partly visible, in the manner of Wijnants, and an unidentified seascape. (See also plates 59–61).

Plate 59
THE LOVE LETTER. Detail: the two figures.

Plate 60
THE LOVE LETTER. Detail: the curtain, the chimney-piece and the two pictures.

Plate 61
THE LOVE LETTER. Detail: the tiled floor and the still life in the foreground.

Plate 62
AN ALLEGORY OF PAINTING ("THE ARTIST'S STUDIO"). *Canvas, 130 × 110. Vienna, Kunsthistorisches Museum.* Signed on the map I ver-meer. Datable between 1665 and 1670. Possibly to be identified with Number 3 in the Amsterdam auction of 1696. A masterpiece of Vermeer's mature period. Listed in the inventory of his possessions and willed to his mother-in-law: it has been described as a "realistic allegory."

The problem of the identity of the artist who turns his back on us is insoluble. He is an anonymous Dutch artist in cap and idealistic festival costume, painting a girl with a laurel wreath on her head, a trumpet in one hand and a book in the other. The girl, with her eyes lowered, has been thought to represent Fame (though not, certainly, a Baroque "Fame"). Now, more reasonably, she is identified as the Muse of History, Clio. But whether Fame or Clio, this coy young woman, her head outlined against the map of the "Seven Provinces" of Holland, seems intended to tell the world of the fame of Dutch painting.

Exceedingly subtle observations have been made about the composition and pictorial structure of the painting, its curious perspective and its intellectual content. The smallest detail has been ingeniously interpreted. But the poetry of *The Artist's Studio* is above all of an optical kind and there is a danger in attempting to read too much "significance" into it. (See also plates 63–66 and color plate IV.)

Plate 63
AN ALLEGORY OF PAINTING ("THE ARTIST'S STUDIO"). Detail.

Plate 64
AN ALLEGORY OF PAINTING ("THE ARTIST'S STUDIO"). Detail: the chandelier.

Color Plate IV
AN ALLEGORY OF PAINTING ("THE ARTIST'S STUDIO"). Detail: the model.

Plate 65
AN ALLEGORY OF PAINTING ("THE ARTIST'S STUDIO"). Detail: the artist.

Plate 66
AN ALLEGORY OF PAINTING ("THE ARTIST'S STUDIO"). Detail: the hand with the trumpet and of the table with still life.

Plate 67
THE GUITAR PLAYER. *Canvas, 50 × 42.5. London, Kenwood House,*

Iveagh Bequest. Signed IVMEER. Dateable between 1665 and 1670. At the time of Vermeer's death the picture belonged to his widow and was made over to the baker in payment of a debt, together with *A Lady Writing a Letter and Her Maid* (plate 74). The work is very sharp and lively in expression. A landscape in the style of Wijnants hangs on the wall. There is an old copy in the Johnson Collection, Philadelphia. (See also plates 68 and 69.)

Plate 68

THE GUITAR PLAYER. Detail: the right hand and the instrument.

Plate 69

THE GUITAR PLAYER. Detail: the head and the picture on the wall.

Plate 70

THE ASTRONOMER. *Canvas, 51 × 45. Paris, Baron Edouard de Rothschild Collection.* Signed and dated MEER MDCLXVIII. On the wall, part of the picture representing *The Finding of Moses* which appears also in *A Lady Writing a Letter and Her Maid.*

Plate 71

THE GEOGRAPHER. *Canvas, 53 × 46.5. Frankfurt-am-Main, Stadelsches Kunstinstitut.* Signed IVMEER. The picture is falsely signed I. ver-MEER MDCLXVIII. Even if, as it would seem, the date was added later, the picture should nevertheless be considered as a kind of pendant to *The Astronomer*, which is in fact dated 1668. The two scientists are certainly represented in the same way. *The Geographer* is not in perfect condition and it has lost its freshness. It is curious that there should be numerous copies of this picture, since Vermeer has in general been very seldom copied. Huyghe toyed with the idea that one of the

artist's sons acted as model for both *The Astronomer* and *The Geographer.* (See also plates 72 and 73.)

Plate 72

THE GEOGRAPHER. Detail: still life.

Plate 73

THE GEOGRAPHER. Detail: the geographer.

Plate 74

A LADY WRITING A LETTER AND HER MAID. *Canvas, 68.5 × 57.5. Johannesburg (or Cape Town), Lady Beit Collection.* Signed IVMEER. Datable between 1665 and 1670. At the time of Vermeer's death the picture belonged to his widow and was made over to the baker in payment of a debt, together with *The Guitar Player* (plate 67). The highly finished surface points to a relatively late period. On the wall, *The Finding of Moses* by an unknown Italianate artist: this picture also appeared in *The Astronomer* (plate 70). It will be remembered that in 1672 Vermeer was summoned as an expert in Italian art to give his opinion in a forgery case. (See also plates 75 and 76.)

Plate 75

A LADY WRITING A LETTER AND HER MAID. Detail: the maid.

Plate 76

A LADY WRITING A LETTER AND HER MAID. Detail: the lady.

Plate 77

A MISTRESS AND MAIDSERVANT. *Canvas, 88 × 76. New York, Frick Collection.* Traces of a signature. Datable between 1665 and 1670. Number 7 in the Amsterdam auction of 1696. A late work, judging from the elaborate hair style. The lady wears the same pale yellow jacket edged with ermine as the woman in *The Love Letter* (plate 58) and the girl in *The Guitar Player* (plate 67). Worth noting is the "dialogue" between the lady and the maid, in keeping with tradition, which Vermeer shows here. As Plietzsch has discovered, the background of the picture was not originally neutral but adorned with a hanging. This must have been painted before 1809, as the picture appears in its present state in an engraving of that year in the Lebrun Collection. (See also plate 78.)

Plate 78
A MISTRESS AND MAIDSERVANT. Detail: the maid.

Plate 79
THE ALLEGORY OF FAITH. *Canvas, 113 × 89. New York, Metropolitan Museum of Art.* Formerly in Moscow. Datable after 1670. Recognized as a work by Vermeer by Max J. Friedländer when it was with an art dealer in Berlin (it was then attributed to Eglon van der Neer): subsequently it passed into the Bredius Collection. The painting was perhaps executed on commission. In order to represent a religious allegory, Vermeer seems to have followed almost to the letter the precepts formulated by Cesare Ripa in his *Iconologia*, which was published in translation in Amsterdam in 1644. The result is that Vermeer has given the figure of Faith the features and dress of a woman lifted straight from the repertoire of Dutch "fine painting," modeling her with languid eyes and conventional gestures. The crucifix (which is not mentioned by Ripa) indicates, according to Swillens, that it is the Catholic Faith which is symbolized. The smooth painting of the figure and the symbols is in marked contrast to the remarkably beautiful Pointillist treatment of the Gobelin

tapestry. The picture of *The Crucifixion* behind the figure seems to be identical with one by Jacob Jordaens now in the Foundation Terningh in Antwerp. (See also plate 80.)

Plate 80
THE ALLEGORY OF FAITH. Detail: the crucifix, the chalice and the Bible.

Plate 81
A YOUNG WOMAN STANDING AT A VIRGINAL. *Canvas, 50 × 45. London, National Gallery.* Signed IVMEER. Datable after 1670. Possibly to be identified with Number 37 in the Amsterdam auction of 1696: but this number could equally refer to *A Young Woman Seated at a Virginal* (plate 85) also in the National Gallery. *A Young Woman Standing at a Virginal* was acquired for the gallery in 1892 at the Thoré-Bürger Sale. Not only the dress and the hair style but the whole "feeling" of the picture and its coldness of handling suggest a late period—perhaps, indeed, the last years of the artist's life. His treatment of the satin dress seems to rival Terborch. Though it appears to mark a decline, the picture shows very considerable subtlety of structure in both composition and color. On the wall hangs a landscape in the style of Wijnants and a *Standing Cupid*, possibly by Caesar van Everdingen, which also appears in *A Girl Asleep* and *The Music Lesson* (plates 9 and 24). (See also plates 82–84.)

Plate 82
A YOUNG WOMAN STANDING AT A VIRGINAL. Detail.

Plate 83
A YOUNG WOMAN STANDING AT A VIRGINAL. Detail: the instrument.

Plate 84

A YOUNG WOMAN STANDING AT A VIRGINAL. Detail: the head.

Plate 85

A YOUNG WOMAN SEATED AT A VIRGINAL. *Canvas, 51 × 45. London, National Gallery.* Signed IVMeer. Acquired for the gallery at the Thoré-Bürger Sale. This work should be considered a pendant to *A Young Woman Standing at a Virginal*. On the wall is Dirk van Baburen's *The Procuress* (Museum of Fine Arts, Boston: replica in the Rijksmuseum, Amsterdam). This also appears in *The Concert* (plate 33). (See also plates 86–88.)

Plate 86

A YOUNG WOMAN SEATED AT A VIRGINAL. Detail: the instrument.

Plate 87

A YOUNG WOMAN SEATED AT A VIRGINAL. Detail: the picture on the wall.

Plate 88

A YOUNG WOMAN SEATED AT A VIRGINAL. Detail: head of the lady and Vermeer's signature.

LOCATION OF PAINTINGS

AMSTERDAM

RIJKSMUSEUM
The Milkmaid (plates 16–17 and color plate II).
The Little Street (plates 18–21).
The Woman in Blue (plates 47–48).
The Love Letter (plates 58–61).

BERLIN

STAATLICHES MUSEEN
A Girl Drinking with a Gentleman (plates 22–23).
The Pearl Necklace (plates 50–51).

BOSTON (MASSACHUSETTS)

ISABELLA STEWART GARDNER MUSEUM
The Concert (plates 33–34).

BRUNSWICK

HERZOG ANTON ULRICH MUSEUM
A Girl with a Glass of Wine and Two Gentlemen (plate 26).

DRESDEN

GEMÄLDEGALERIE
The Procuress (plates 5–8).
A Lady Reading a Letter by the Window (plates 12–13).

EDINBURGH

NATIONAL GALLERY OF SCOTLAND
Christ in the House of Martha and Mary (plates 2–4).

FRANKFURT-AM-MAIN

STADELSCHES KUNSTINSTITUT
The Geographer (plates 71–73).

THE HAGUE

MAURITSHUIS
Diana and the Nymphs (plate 1 and color plate I).
View of Delft (plates 40–45).
Girl in a Turban (color plate III and plate 49).

JOHANNESBURG (or Cape Town)

LADY BEIT COLLECTION
A Lady Writing a Letter and Her Maid (plates 74–76).

LONDON

BUCKINGHAM PALACE
A Gentleman and Lady at a Spinet (plates 27–32).
KENWOOD HOUSE
The Guitar Player (plates 67–69).
NATIONAL GALLERY
A Young Woman Standing at a Virginal (plates 81–84).
A Young Woman Seated at a Virginal (plates 85–88).

NASSAU (BAHAMAS)

LADY OAKES COLLECTION
A Lady Writing a Letter (plate 53).

NEW YORK

METROPOLITAN MUSEUM OF ART
A Girl Asleep (plates 9–11).
A Young Woman with a Water Jug (plates 35–37).
The Lute Player (plate 52).
The Allegory of Faith (plates 79–80).
FRICK COLLECTION
A Soldier and Laughing Girl (plates 14–15).
The Music Lesson (plates 24–25).
A Mistress and Maidservant (plates 77–78).
MR AND MRS CHARLES B. WRIGHTSON COLLECTION.
Head of a Girl (plate 46).

PARIS

LOUVRE
The Lacemaker (plates 54–55).
ROTHSCHILD COLLECTION
The Astronomer (plate 70).

VIENNA

KUNSTHISTORISCHES MUSEUM
An Allegory of Painting ("The Artist's Studio") (plates 62–66 and color plate IV).

WASHINGTON, D.C.

NATIONAL GALLERY OF ART
A Woman Weighing Pearls (plates 38–39).
A Girl with a Red Hat (plate 56).
A Girl with a Flute (plate 57).

SELECTED CRITICISM

So died that phoenix (Carel Fabritius) in his thirtieth year, // In the middle and at the height of his life; // But happily his flame ignited // Vermeer who, as a master, perpetuated his knowledge.

ARNOLD BON,
Dirck Evertsz. van Bleysweyck, *Beschrijvinge de Stadt Delft*, Delft, 1667.

In order to see a painting by Van der Meer, I traveled hundreds of miles; to obtain a reproduction of a Van der Meer I committed numberless follies.

W. BÜRGER (E. J. Th. Thoré),
Van Der Meer de Delft, 1866.

So, do you know an artist called Vermeer who, for example, painted a very lovely pregnant Dutch woman? This strange painter's palette consists of blue, lemon yellow, pearl gray, black and white. Of course, a few rare pictures do have all the rich colors of a complete palette. But the combination of lemon yellow, pale blue and pearl gray is as characteristic of him as black, white, gray and pink is of Velazquez. . . .

VAN GOGH,
Letter to Emile Bernard, July 1888.

His work is the crystallization of our art of the seventeenth century. It can be said of this strange artist that he was perhaps the most characteristically Dutch, and at the same time the most Greek, of all the old Dutch masters. The shining texture of his vibrant, enameled color surface renders the noble splendor of light itself, but he imbued this splendor with the serene majesty of a truly epic art.

Calm, meditative and domestic, this imperturbable pearl-fisher of most mature and perfect craft must doubtless have been;

43

but unlike so many of this school, who nursed and tended their pictures with minute patience, he is everywhere large, never homespun in anything he painted.

JAN VETH,
In the Shadow of the Old Masters, 1911.

Observe how the Pisan [Orazio Gentileschi] reaches a more precise and circumstantial definition of interior space: the action of light is more delicate and true, richer in transitions along the scale of luminosity and transparency. This construction of an interior as a lucid pictorial space which gives form and color, substance and surface—the construction which will be carried to its ultimate pitch of refinement by Pieter de Hoogh and Jan Vermeer—finds here in Gentileschi an Italian pathway between the quick-tempered Caravaggio and neat, clear-sighted and *bourgeois* Holland.

R. LONGHI,
"Gentileschi, padre e figlia," in *L'Arte,* 1916.

In any case, as an artist he had already lived long enough although he died young in years. One is reminded of Ophelia's words: "O, what a noble mind is here o'erthrown."

P. JOHANSEN,
"Jan Vermeer van Delft," in *Oud Holland,* 1920.

But having read a critic who said that in the *View of Delft* by Vermeer (lent by the museum at The Hague for a Dutch exhibition)—a picture that he loved and thought he knew extremely well—there was a little strip of yellow wall (which he did not, after all, remember) that was so beautifully painted that, considered on its own, it seemed like an exquisite Chinese work of art, with a beauty of its own, Bergotte ate a few potatoes, and went out to the exhibition. . . .

You told me that you had seen some pictures by Vermeer. You realize, of course, that they are all fragments of the same world: a world that is always—with whatever genius it is re-created—made up of the same table, the same rug, the same woman, the same fresh and unique beauty. He is an enigma in an epoch in which nothing resembled nor explained him; and he can only be explained if you do not try to connect him to the others through his subjects, but try to isolate the particular impression that his color produces.

MARCEL PROUST,
La Prisonnière, 1923.

Take his *Girl in a Turban*—as for the grace of the model, the pure, smooth enamel of the finish, the unusual and exquisite harmony of the yellows and blues framing the divine face—these are qualities that only Vermeer could feel and express. And the blue and white soft, ethereal charm, the innocent, pure enjoyment of ornamentation brings to mind the beauty of a majolica plate—this quality the artist owed to the pottery makers of his country.

L. GILLET,
L'Art hollandais au Jeu de Paume, 1921.

In everything that Vermeer painted there lies in suspension, as it were, an atmosphere of childhood recollection, a dream-like peace, a complete stillness, an almost elegiac clarity which is too refined to be described as melancholy. Is this realism?

On closer inspection one realizes that these are not Dutch women of the year sixteen hundred and such and such, but figures from an elegiac dream-world of utter peace and tranquility.

J. HUIZINGA,
Dutch Culture of the Seventeenth Century, Dutch edition, 1941.

You have been waiting to hear his name for a long time: Vermeer of Delft. And as I say it, I am sure that his stimulating juxtaposition of heavenly blue and limpid yellow as pure as Arabia immediately comes to your mind, like the colors on a coat of arms! But I do not want to talk to you here about colors, despite their quality and interplay—so coldly exact that they seem to have been obtained by pure intellect rather than by a brush. What fascinates me is his pure, uncluttered and sterilized vision, cleansed of all matter: a vision that has an almost mathematical or angelic clarity—more simply, photographic. But what a photograph! This artist is enclosed within the lens of his camera and from there he captures the outside world. We can only compare the result with the delicate marvels of the dark-room and the first appearance on daguerrotype plates of figures drawn by a hand more sure and incisive than even Holbein's: I mean by the rays of the sun.

PAUL CLAUDEL,
L'Oeil Ecoute, 1946.

He observed life as a still-life painter. A copy after Steen is at least a tolerable illustration: a copy after Vermeer—it is significant that they practically don't exist, only falsifications—is a complete nonentity.

MAX J. FRIEDLÄNDER,
Essays, 1947.

Had he lived in the fifteenth century, he would have belonged to the great Primitives. . . . In his moments of fullness, Vermeer was able to penetrate and conquer the visible world to an extent and depth that we still cannot fathom.

A. B. DE VRIES,
Jan Vermeer de Delft, 1948.

Vermeer is also one of the most perfect symbols of his time and his country; his universe is secret, impenetrable and dominated by his ego. His poetry is steeped in his own epoch, draws all its strength from it—but only in order to reach the summit where it is isolated from, and dominates the forest below.

The two opposed aspirations of European painting are present in him, just as they are in Van Eyck, and for the same reason. These are the sense of the transient nature of things, which Northern naturalism seizes on the wing, and the sense of a perfection linked to eternity, toward which all the will of Mediterranean intellectualism is turned. The melancholy sense of the passage of time, of all that escapes with the vanishing moment—those half-glimpsed profiles, the souls in suspension, the hours slipping inexorably by with the sun and the light on the wall, the disappearing day, the already visible shadow—all this is as devastating in Vermeer's still small rooms as it is among the wind and driving clouds of Ruysdael. We know this: that what is now so intensely and vividly present will never be again. At the very moment the artist transmits the image to us from beyond the grave, it is no more.

RENÉ HUYGHE,
La Poétique de Vermeer, 1948.

But in one instance the rendering of atmosphere reached a point of perfection that for sheer accuracy has never been surpassed: Vermeer's *View of Delft*. This unique work is certainly the nearest painting which has ever come to a colored photograph. Not only has Vermeer an uncannily true sense of tone, but he has used it with an almost inhuman detachment. He has not allowed any one point in the scene to engage his interest, but has set down everything with a complete evenness of focus. Such, at least, is our first impression of the picture, and the basis of its popularity with those who do not normally care for paintings. But the more we study the *View of Delft* the more artful it becomes, the more carefully calculated its design, the more consistent all its components. No doubt truth of tone adds to our delight, but this could not sustain us long without other qualities, and perhaps could not, by itself, have reached such a point of perfection, for the mood of heightened receptivity necessary to achieve it cannot be isolated from that tension of spirit which goes to the creation of any great work of art.

SIR KENNETH CLARK,
Landscape into Art, 1949.

Like the most beautiful frescoes at Pompeii, and like Seurat's *Parade*, *The Love Letter* has been carefully relegated to the gold class. Objects and persons are arranged in constant relationship and are identified with the surrounding architecture without ever losing their personality. With all due respect to the abstract painters, this is a miracle.

ANDRÉ LHOTE,
Traité de la figure, 1950.

The lack of facility in dealing with human issues, which emerges side by side with the elemental clarity of vision which is its counterpart is the fundamental factor in the formation of his style. The lack itself is a common one. Vermeer's distinction is that, with the passivity characteristic of his thought, he accepted this part of his nature as a basis of the expressive content of his style. The instinctive seriousness of his assent to the requirements of his temperament is the sign of his genius.

LAWRENCE GOWING,
Vermeer, 1952.

BIBLIOGRAPHICAL NOTE

A complete bibliography for Vermeer will be found in E. Trautscholdt's article in vol. xxxiv of Thieme-Becker, *Kunstlerlexikon*, 1940; in A.B. De Vries, *Jan Vermeer de Delft*, 1948; and in P. T. A. Swillens, *Johannes Vermeer*, 1950.

Of the articles which have appeared since 1950, the most significant are those which deal with the interpretation of *An Allegory of Painting*; in particular those by Professor Sedelmayer in *Zeitschrift für Professor Jantzen*, 1952, and Charles de Tolnay in the *Gazette des Beaux-Arts*, April 1953.

The following is only a selection of the monographs and most important essays on Vermeer.

W. BÜRGER (E. J. Th. Thoré). *Van der Meer de Delft*, Paris, 1866.
C. HOFSTEDE DE GROOT. *Beschreibendes und Kritisches Verzeichnis der Werke der hervorragendsten holländischen Maler des XVII Jahrhunderts*, Esslingen-Paris, 1907.
C. HOFSTEDE DE GROOT. *Jan Vermeer van Delft en Carel Fabritius*, Amsterdam, 1907–30.
E. V. LUCAS. *Vermeer of Delft*, London, 1922.
P. L. HALE. *Jan Vermeer of Delft*, Boston, 1937.
E. PLIETZSCH. *Vermeer van Delft*, Monaco, 1939.
A. B. DE VRIES. *Jan Vermeer de Delft, suivi de "La Poétique de Vermeer" par René Huyghe*, Paris, 1948.
P. T. A. SWILLENS. *Johannes Vermeer*, Utrecht-Brussels, 1950.
L. GOWING. *Vermeer*, London, 1952.
A. MALRAUX. *Vermeer*, Paris, 1952.

Essays
J. VETH. *Im Schatten alter Kunst*, Berlin, 1911.
H. VOSS. "Vermeer van Delft und die Utrechter Schule," in *Monatshefte für Kunstwissenschaft*, 1912.
P. JOHANSEN. "Jan Vermeer de Delft," in *Oud-Holland*, 1920.
W. R. VALENTINER. "Zum 300. Geburtstag Jan Vermeers," in *Pantheon*, 1932.
R. HUYGHE. "Vermeer et Proust," in *L'Amour de l'Art*, 1936.
E. TRAUTSCHOLDT in Thieme-Becker, *Kunstlerlexikon*, vol. xxxiv, 1940.
A. J. J. M. VAN PEER. "Drie collecties schilderijen van Jan Vermeer," in *Oud-Holland*, 1957.
J. G. VAN GELDER. *De schilderkunst van Jan Vermeer (met commentaar van J. E. Emmens)*, Utrecht, 1958.
J. Q. VAN REGTEREN ALTENA. "Een jeugdwerk van Johannes Vermeer," in *Oud-Holland*, 1960.
A. P. DE MIRIMONDE. "Les sujets musicaux chez Vermeer de Delft," in *Gazette des Beaux-Arts*, 1961.

REPRODUCTIONS

ACKNOWLEDGEMENT FOR
PLATES

Mauritshuis, The Hague: plates 1, 40–41, 42–44; *National Gallery of Scotland, Edinburgh:* plates 2–4; *F. Bruckmann A.-G., Munich:* plate 5–8, 12–13, 71–73; *Metropolitan Museum of Art, New York:* plates 9–11, 35–37, 52; *Frick Collection, New York:* plates 14–15, 24–25, 77–78; *Rijksmuseum, Amsterdam:* plates 16–23, 47–48, 58–60, 62–66; *Walter Dräyer, Zürich:* plate 26; *National Gallery, London:* plates 27–32, 74–76, 81–88; *Isabella Stewart Gardner Museum, Boston:* plates 33–34; *National Gallery of Art, Washington, D.C.:* plates 38–39, 56–57; *Archives Centrales Iconographiques, Brussels:* plates 45, 61; *Charles Uht, Brussels:* plate 46; *Rijksbureau voor Kunsthistorie, The Hague:* plate 49; *Staatliches Museen, Berlin:* plates 50–51; *Oakes Collection, Nassau:* plate 53; *Vizzavona, Paris:* plates 54–55; *Iveagh Bequest, Kenwood House, London:* plates 67–69; *Rothschild Collection, Paris:* plate 70; *A Dingjan, The Hague:* plates 79–80.

DIANA AND THE NYMPHS,
The Hague, Mauritshuis
(*detail of plate 1*)

Plate I. DIANA AND THE NYMPHS,
The Hague, Mauritshuis

Plate 2. CHRIST IN THE HOUSE OF MARTHA AND MARY,
Edinburgh, National Gallery of Scotland

Plate 3. *Detail of plate 2*

Plate 4. *Detail of plate 2*

Plate 5. THE PROCURESS,
Dresden, Gemäldegalerie

Plate 6. *Detail of plate 5*

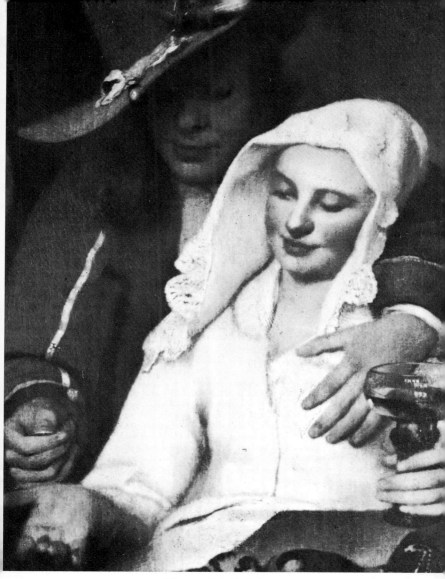

Plate 7. *Detail of plate 5*

Plate 8. *Detail of plate 5*

Plate 9. A GIRL ASLEEP,
New York, Metropolitan Museum of Art

Plate 10. *Detail of plate 9*

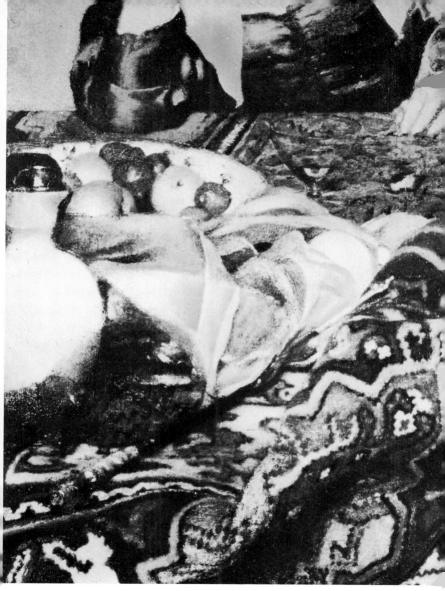

Plate 11. *Detail of plate 9*

Plate 12. A LADY READING A LETTER BY THE WINDOW,
Dresden, Gemäldegalerie

Plate 13. *Detail of plate 12*

Plate 14. A SOLDIER AND LAUGHING GIRL,
New York, Frick Collection

Plate 15. *Detail of plate 14*

Plate 16. THE MILKMAID,
Amsterdam, Rijksmuseum

THE MILKMAID,
Amsterdam, Rijksmuseum
(*detail of plate 16*)

Plate 17. *Detail of plate 16*

Plate 18. THE LITTLE STREET,
Amsterdam, Rijksmuseum

Plate 19. *Detail of plate 18*

Plate 20. *Detail of plate 18*

Plate 21. *Detail of plate 18*

Plate 22. A GIRL DRINKING WITH A GENTLEMAN,
Berlin, Staatliches Museen

Plate 23. *Detail of plate 22*

Plate 24. THE MUSIC LESSON,
New York, Frick Collection

Plate 25. *Detail of plate 24*

Plate 26. A GIRL WITH A GLASS OF WINE AND TWO
GENTLEMEN,
Brunswick, Herzog Anton Ulrich Museum

Plate 27. A GENTLEMAN AND LADY AT A SPINET,
London, Buckingham Palace

Plate 28. *Detail of plate 27*

Plate 29. *Detail of plate 27*

Plate 30. *Detail of plate 27*

Plate 31. *Detail of plate 27*

Plate 32. *Detail of plate 27*

Plate 33. THE CONCERT,
Boston, Isabella Stewart Gardner Museum

Plate 34. *Detail of plate 33*

Plate 35. A YOUNG WOMAN WITH A WATER JUG,
New York, Metropolitan Museum of Art

Plate 36. *Detail of plate 35*

Plate 37. Detail of plate 35

Plate 38. A WOMAN WEIGHING PEARLS,
Washington, D.C., National Gallery of Art

Plate 39. *Detail of plate 38*

Plates 40–41.
The Hag

:W OF DELFT,
Mauritshuis

Plate 42. *Detail of plates 40–41*

Plate 43. *Detail of plates 40–41*

Plate 44. *Detail of plates 40–41*

Plate 45. *Detail of plates 40–41*

Plate 46. HEAD OF A GIRL,
New York, Mr and Mrs Charles B. Wrightson Collection

Plate 47. THE WOMAN IN BLUE
Amsterdam, Rijksmuseum

Plate 48. *Detail of plate 47*

GIRL IN A TURBAN,
The Hague, Mauritshuis

Plate 50. THE PEARL NECKLACE,
Berlin, Staatliches Museen

GIRL IN A TURBAN,
The Hague, Mauritshuis

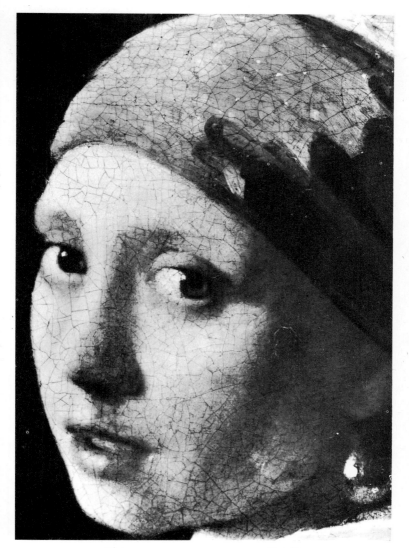

Plate 49. GIRL IN A TURBAN (*detail*)
The Hague, Mauritshuis

Plate 50. THE PEARL NECKLACE,
Berlin, Staatliches Museen

Plate 51. *Detail of plate 50*

Plate 52. THE LUTE PLAYER,
New York, Metropolitan Museum of Art

Plate 53. A LADY WRITING A LETTER,
Nassau (Bahamas), Lady Oakes Collection

Plate 54. THE LACEMAKER,
Paris, Louvre

Plate 55. *Detail of plate 54*

Plate 56. A GIRL WITH A RED HAT,
Washington, D.C., National Gallery of Art

Plate 57. A GIRL WITH A FLUTE,
Washington, D.C., National Gallery of Art

Plate 58. THE LOVE LETTER,
Amsterdam, Rijksmuseum

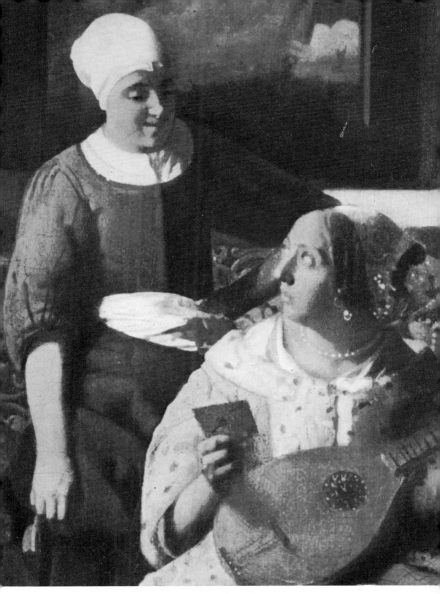

Plate 59. *Detail of plate 58*

Plate 60. *Detail of plate 58*

Plate 61. *Detail of plate 58*

Plate 62. AN ALLEGORY OF PAINTING ("The Artist's Studio")
Vienna, Kunsthistorisches Museum

Plate 63. *Detail of plate 62*

Plate 64. *Detail of plate 62*

AN ALLEGORY OF PAINTING,
Vienna, Kunsthistorisches Museum
(detail of plate 62)

Plate 66. *Detail of plate 62*

AN ALLEGORY OF PAINTING,
Vienna, Kunsthistorisches Museum
(*detail of plate 62*)

Plate 65. *Detail of plate 62*

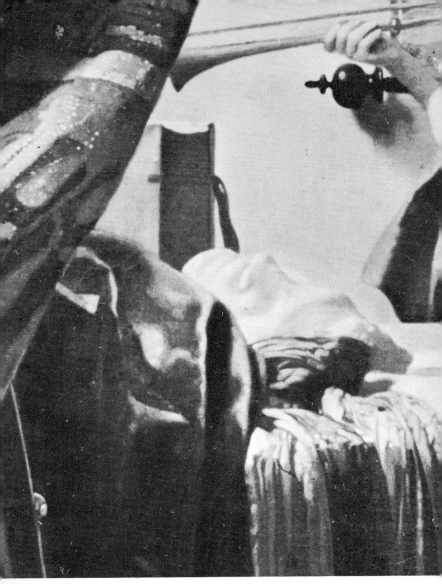

Plate 66. *Detail of plate 62*

Plate 67. THE GUITAR PLAYER,
London, Kenwood House

Plate 68. *Detail of plate 67*

Plate 69. *Detail of plate 67*

Plate 70. THE ASTRONOMER,
Paris, Rothschild Collection

Plate 71. THE GEOGRAPHER,
Frankfurt-am-Main, Stadelsches Kunstinstitut

Plate 72. *Detail of plate 71*

Plate 73. *Detail of plate 71*

Plate 74. A LADY WRITING A LETTER AND HER MAID,
Johannesburg (or Cape Town), Lady Beit Collection

Plate 75. *Detail of plate 74*

Plate 76. *Detail of plate 74*

Plate 77. A MISTRESS AND MAIDSERVANT,
New York, Frick Collection

Plate 78. *Detail of plate 77*

Plate 79. THE ALLEGORY OF FAITH,
New York, Metropolitan Museum of Art

Plate 80. *Detail of plate 79*

Plate 81. A YOUNG WOMAN STANDING AT A VIRGINAL
London, National Gallery

Plate 82. *Detail of plate 81*

Plate 83. *Detail of plate 81*

Plate 84. *Detail of plate 81*

Plate 85. A YOUNG WOMAN SEATED AT A VIRGINAL,
London, National Gallery

Plate 86. *Detail of plate 85*

Plate 87. *Detail of plate 85*

Plate 88. *Detail of plate 85*